101 Wedding Planning Tips

To save you time, stress, and money!

Written By: Jason J. Kelley

Illustrated by: Mikiyah Jo Kelley

Dedication

This book is dedicated to my wife Laura. If it wasn't for her interest in the wedding industry all those years ago, I may not be writing this book today. After expressing her interest in wedding planning, she studied for several months to become a certified wedding planner. Following her lead, I then studied and trained to convert my DJing and Entertainment skills in to being a Professional Wedding DJ. Since then we have not only lived together, but have worked together growing our family and our business.

They say behind every good man is a good woman. That statement could not be more true. Without my wife's constant efforts towards our family, our business, and my sanity, my life would be an extremely chaotic mess full of sticky notes and randomness. Anyone that knows me, knows that I am a bit of a scatter brain. My mind is constantly thinking of new objectives, creative ideas, and solutions that can possibly make subjects better. I have lists upon lists of projects I want to work on, half ideas, and sentence fragments pertaining to many different areas of my notes. Amongst all of that chaos, was the idea of writing a book to help brides and grooms throughout their planning process. Once again, my amazing wife has put her love and effort into our family and has booked us a 5 night cruise for a vacation this year. This has been just the break I needed to sit down and finally put this book together for you. I only worked on it during downtime on our vacation (flights, uber rides, mornings when the family is sleeping, etc.) in order to still enjoy my time with family. The time away from social media and business was very much a mental refresher for me. Thank you Laura for always knowing exactly what I need. The life we have lived together and inside the wedding industry has been an amazing journey of heart warming experiences, stressful situations, and fun. I'm truly blessed to have someone as amazing as you to share so much with every day.

Preface

Weddings are very much an amazing experience filled with love, emotion, and lots of unforgettable memories. For these reasons and more, I have devoted my life to not only being an amazing Wedding DJ, but an overall Wedding Professional. After thousands of weddings serviced by our company, working with hundreds of professional (and not so professional) wedding service providers, I have learned the ins and outs of weddings. I am dedicated to sharing my knowledge and expertise with each and every bride and groom that I encounter, whether they hire any of our services or not. Therefore, I have decided to put together a list of tips, advice, and secrets that will help anyone in one way or another while planning a wedding. There are a lot of tips not covered in this book, and also a lot of insight in to the wedding industry I would like to share with you, but if I included it all in to one book you may just feel overwhelmed with information.

All of the tips you'll find in this book have derived from both Personal Opinion and Professional Experiences. Every wedding is different because every couple is different. Therefore every wedding planning process will also be different. These tips have been created to help most couples through the daunting and sometimes energy draining process that comes with planning a wedding. You're sure to find at least several of these tips helpful, but keep in mind they are not designed to be an absolutely perfected planning process.

Even after all of the efforts I have put in on a daily basis to be the Wedding Professional I am, I still make it a point to find quality time to spend with my family. Family is what keeps me driven each and every day. Being a family man, I could think of no better artist than my 8 year old daughter Mikiyah Jo to lend her talents to illustrating this book for you. We had a lot of fun putting together these images for your enjoyment. Family is very important and our family is extremely glad these tips have found you while you are beginning to build a family of your own. So from our family to yours, we want to say Congratulations and Enjoy!

Table Of Contents

1. Extend Your Engagement Period And Plan

There's nothing wrong
with having a longer
engagement. You are
already with the person
you want to spend the
rest of your life with, there
should be no hurry to tie

the knot. If you pick an extended date and give
yourself some extra time to plan, you will thank
yourself in the long run. Taking the time to really
plan everything out will be a lot less stressful. Also,
the farther out you book some service providers,
the better the possibility of receiving a discounted
rate. You may even avoid any extra cost if they plan
to increase their prices. If you are able to save a
date with a wedding service provider that
accommodates lengthy engagements, make sure
they agree to a locked in rate for their services that

won't be susceptible to any price increases or additional fees.

2. Choosing A Date For Your Wedding

Most areas in the united states have an "Off Season". That's basically a few months when weddings are not as plentiful. If you plan your wedding date within that time frame, you are more likely to receive discounts and save a lot of money in your wedding budget. Also Fridays and Sundays tend to be days that will save you money as well. Try not to plan your wedding for a major holiday. A lot of guests may not be able to attend and you may have to pay extra costs with your service professionals you decide on for your big day. Keep in mind if it's a popular date you are going to want to be on top of everything much more to ensure you will be able to hire the service professionals you want. This year 8-18-18 was a very popular date and filled up very quickly. In the Greater Toledo

Area, there are over 5,000 weddings annually. That means there will also be other brides and grooms planning their weddings on the same date you select. Keep that in mind when planning your wedding and you'll be able to appreciate the importance of prompt planning.

3. Create A Planning Timeline Once You Select A Date.

It is no secret that there is a lot of details and emotions that go in to planning a wedding. By taking the time ahead of time to give yourself a schedule for your planning process, you'll ensure nothing gets put off and avoid any unnecessary stress. Staying organized is key to a stress free planning process. It is best to start right away and break things down month by month of what you will need to confirm and plan. Look into purchasing a wedding planner book or binder that has all of these timelines already broken down for you. There are also a few user friendly websites and apps designed to help you throughout the planning process. We also hope this book will assist your planning efforts to ensure everything goes even smoother for you.

4. Set A Budget

Weddings can be very expensive and easily become unnecessarily expensive if you're not taking the time to plan appropriately. The only way to track how much you're saving by being diligent and frugal is to set a reasonable budget. Figure out your top end of your budget in order to avoid not exceeding that threshold. By doing some research online you'll be able to figure out an average price for each wedding professional service in your general area to know what to expect. Keep in mind there will be some elements that you'll want to go higher than average based on the service provider and how important that element is to you. It is ok to go outside your budget a little for important services, as long as you can balance the additional cost from another area of your budget.

5. The Credit Card Advantage

Although we absolutely do not want to encourage anyone to get into any sort of credit card debt. There are credit card options out there that offer some great rewards that you can take advantage of for your wedding purchases. A lot of credit cards have a 12 month no interest option with cash back rewards. If you are already paying a lot of money for your wedding, make your money work for you. Some credit cards also offer airline miles that you can rack up and potentially use for your honeymoon travels. The credit card advantage tip is only encouraged if you are able to pay off your purchases in a timely manner and avoid any unnecessary fees. Use this tip responsibly and you'll save as well as earn.

6. Don't Get Sucked Into Traditions

Let's face it the times have changed since your parents and grandparents planned their weddings. A lot of modern brides and grooms are not only planning their wedding themselves, but also paying for everything themselves. There are a lot of traditional wedding elements that you can avoid that will help you minimize your planning process as well as save you unnecessary additional costs in your budget. Don't be afraid to be non traditional even if outside parties are pressuring you to do so. Remember this is your wedding, you can be as creative and personalize as much as you want in order for you and your fiancé to have a wedding that you will remember forever.

7. Prioritize Your Expectations

Throughout your planning process, no matter how much you plan and what you expect, many things will fluctuate. That includes your budget itself. Make sure you set guidelines for yourself and stick to those boundaries. It is very beneficial to set priorities on not only which professional wedding service and wedding elements are most important to you, but also how much wiggle room you're willing to give your budget for each element for your wedding, and even how many guests you are willing to invite and pay for to attend your wedding. Organize a list of wedding services and wedding elements in order of high priority to low priority and it will help you with negotiations and budget adjustments without setting yourself up to be in over your head in areas that are not of great importance to you personally. This should be done before a lot of your research to make sure you stay focused on what you and your fiancé want and to avoid being "talked in to" or "sold" on anything that you weren't expecting.

8. Take Notes At Weddings

If you're planning your wedding and you also get invited to a wedding, it can be beneficial for you to make sure to attend. Being a guest at a wedding will potentially help you with your planning process. A great way to figure out some aspects you may want for your big day and also eliminate the things you do not want is by attending weddings and experiencing them first hand. You might think you want tall center pieces on some of your tables but then quickly realize that it can be difficult for guests to see around them. Whether you're taking actual notes or simply making mental notes, be sure to do it discreetly. You do not want to come off as a snob at your friend or family member's wedding by pointing out all of the things you don't like. Remember it is their big day. But you can absolutely have a great learning experience for your big day by simply taking note of everything you learn. Keep a notepad on your phone, make mental notes of things, and when you've got time, type out a few words for each element you like or don't like. You're also going to want to do that discreetly, you don't want to be that guest that is just on their phone the whole time. If your fiancé is attending with you, have them do the same in order to double up your research. Remember to enjoy yourself too, it's not just a research mission. Your friend or family member just got married and it is a wedding. Weddings are fun.

9. The "Three Major Reasons" Theory

After all of the weddings I have experienced, I've established a "Three Major Reasons" theory. It's pretty simple, people typically go to weddings for 3 major reasons… To Drink, To Eat, and To Dance. If you can keep these things in mind, your guests will have a great time. The way it typically goes is to get them drinking as soon as they get there (Cocktail Hour), get them eating once the bride and groom get there (Dinner), and get them dancing after the dance floor has been blessed (Your First Dance, Father Daughter Dance, Mother Son Dance). If you can ensure your guests enjoy these three elements, your wedding day will definitely be memorable and fun.

10. Consider Reducing Your Guest List

One of your biggest cost factors when planning a wedding is your guest list. You may start out planning your wedding and wanting everyone you know to definitely be invited. However, once you start putting everything together you'll quickly realize that your guests are one of the biggest expenses for your budget. The average price per guest is approximately $50-$75 for food, beverages, napkin, chair, chair cover, guest favor, and anything else you would like to provide for them. By reducing your guest list, you can save quite a bit on your overall budget.

11. Don't Take It Personally If Guests Can't Attend

There may be certain family members or close friends that you miss and really would like to come experience your wedding day with you. Sometimes life gets in the way of plans and  they just may not be able to attend. The best thing to do is to understand first and foremost that by them not being able to attend they are also saving you money, and secondly to not take it personally. Your wedding day is about you and your fiancé starting your family together. If there's an extremely important person that cannot attend and it really does bother or upset you, you can create an option to have someone set up Skype or any form of video chat. Then you will be able to see them and they still get a chance to chat with you for a few moments on your big day. Even though they won't be there physically, you will still be able to have that memory with them as well.

12. Social Media & Email Reminders

We live in a day and age where just about everything is digital. Sending out paper save the dates and invitations is absolutely customary, but you can do even more to ensure your guests don't miss out on your big day. You're spending a lot of money on each guest that has RSVP'd in order for them to eat, drink, and enjoy themselves at your reception. You're sure to have some people RSVP then not show up and unfortunately you've just wasted that money for nothing. You may even have some people forget to RSVP until the last minute and still want to attend your wedding. Creating a

Facebook Group or Facebook Event can be viewed by some as tacky or unconventional. However, it may just be the reminder tool some people need in order to make sure your planning and money has not gone to waste. Gathering up emails and sending out reminders is also a great way to ensure people stay in the loop. There are several options for mass emailing online that are free. Taking the time to contact your guest list through several different forms of communication will be a big help with confirming your actual guest count.

13. Create A Separate Email Address

During your wedding planning process, you'll be signing up for deals, specials, and providing contact information to a lot of different wedding service providers. You may also want to sign up for online deals with wedding websites and e-commerce sites. In order to avoid clogging up your already used email addresses, or missing something because your current email address gets a lot of spam already, you should create a new email address specifically for your wedding. That way when all is said and done, you can just delete or no longer use that email and you won't be bombarded with emails for weddings when you're already married.

14. Create A Webpage Or Website

If you really want your guests to be informed on what to expect for your big day, set up a webpage or website. You can either search your local area for someone to set this up for you fairly inexpensively, or utilize websites like WIX.com. There are several domain providers online that have free webpage options you can utilize. The best thing about this option is that you can include maps and directions to locations, your dinner menu, children policies, contact numbers, hotel accommodation information, and so much more all in one place. Your guests will be that much more informed and there will be less room for any confusion that may arise to stress anyone out. Making everything that much more fun.

15. Create A Hashtag

Almost everyone is on Social Media these days. By creating a personalized hashtag for your big day, all of your guests that post pics and updates from your wedding can all be located in one place. You'll need to research hashtags ahead of time to ensure nobody else has used your hashtag. You wouldn't want your fun mixed up with another wedding's fun. Creating a hashtag is easier than most people think. You just think of it and start using it. It's that simple. You can even include the hashtag information on your invitations, if you would like to prepare everyone ahead of time. Then make sure you have some sort of signage displaying your hashtag at your reception to remind guests to use it. You can even have your DJ or Emcee announce reminders for guests to use it. The hashtag option is a great way to see what your guests are enjoying about your big day as well as seeing all those wonderful memories again even after the celebration has ended.

16. Registering For Gifts

You can expect to receive some pretty great gifts for your wedding day if you have fun with it. You're most likely going to get the towels, kitchen items, and dish ware that you register for. Those items are most common and easy to come by. But, don't be afraid to get creative. If you don't put it on there, you're definitely not going to get it. My wife and I put a lot of random great gift ideas on our registry and actually ended up getting quite a few of them (a sewing machine, an espresso maker, and even a popcorn machine). Remember to add things that both of you can enjoy. It is such a great experience to open presents and get some of the things you really wanted. It just makes your wedding planning that much more worth it.

17. Actual Wedding Nightmares

If you google "Wedding Nightmares" you'll see a lot of horror stories that people have experienced on their wedding day. By putting attention in to your planning process to avoid any mishaps you'll likely be able to avoid a lot of the common mistakes that people have made. However, what you may not find information on is actual wedding nightmares that brides and grooms have prior to the big day. It is very common to have wedding planning nightmares. They typically have nothing to do with your relationship with your fiancé or how well your planning process is going. There is a lot of stress and anxiety that builds up for this day and it can feel overwhelming sometimes. So the nightmares of the cake not arriving, or your dress getting torn, or even nobody showing up to your wedding, are absolutely something that is normal. Don't try to over think them, and definitely don't let them stress you out even more. It's best to just shake them off and keep up with your planning process. A great suggestion is to keep your wedding planning binder by your bed, so if you do have a bad dream that seems to stress you out, you can wake up and feel comfortable knowing you're on top of the planning process. Or if you have to add something of concern to your notes, it'll be easily accessible.

18. Prepare Yourself Mentally

Your emotions are going to run wild leading up to and even on the day of your wedding. Try not to allow yourself to get sucked in to anything negative. You're going to have a lot of people wanting to talk to you and wanting to share their emotions with you as well. You've also spent a lot of time, effort, and money on planning this day, keep in mind not everything will go as perfectly as planned. If you can keep an open mind and enjoy yourself, the small things will not become big things and you will have a much better time! This is also another reason to make sure you hire professionals for your big day. Top Wedding Professionals will be prepared to handle things and adapt to any situations as they happen. Try and remember that at the end of the day, you are married to the one you want to spend the rest of your life with. Goal Accomplished. Everything else you most likely don't have much control over and it's best to not sweat the small stuff.

19. Slimming Down

Most brides want to be in the best shape ever and look as amazing as

possible. There are many ways to help you with weight loss along your journey to the big day. The best point of advice to give is consistency. There are too many diet and exercise programs to list and compare within the pages of this book. I know my wife attests to hiring a personal trainer that will take the time to personalize a plan for you and follow up to make sure you are sticking with that plan. Whatever works best for you, just make sure you follow through with it and you'll be looking and feeling great on your wedding day. Remember, just like anything else that is worth anything, it'll take time. So the earlier you begin your weight loss program, the better results you will have by the day of your wedding.

20. Wedding Emergency Kit

Create a wedding emergency kit (or designate someone responsible enough to handle this task). You'll never know what to expect the day of. Having an emergency kit will be a godsend. Great things to put in this kit are: A tide stick, antacids, headache medicine, a small sewing kit, bandaids, safety pins, touch up make up, even some crackers or a small snack, hairspray, bobby pins, deodorant, and mints. You'll thank yourself in the long run if you need to use any of the items you've prepared in order to keep things from falling apart.

21. Your Marriage License

Make sure you have the right documents ahead of time before going to get your marriage license. If not it can become frustrating. Either call or look up online a list of the information needed at your local court house for obtaining a marriage license. Sometimes obtaining specific documents can take an extended amount of time so make sure you plan accordingly. Also make sure you follow up with your officiant (or whoever you put in charge of this) to ensure that your marriage license has been filed after your wedding.

22. Prepare A Contact List

It is very important to have all of the phone numbers in one place for everyone that has been designate to handle elements for your wedding day. Include contact information for your photographer, florist, dj, caterer, and even parents. By having all of the contact information all gathered on to one list, it will be much easier to handle any situation that may go wrong. It is also important to send this contact list to all wedding professionals in case they need to contact each other for any reason and they can avoid bothering you with simple questions. If you hire a good wedding planner for your day of coordination, they'll most likely handle this for you.

23. Don't Forget About Your Pets

If you have pets that will need looking after, you will want to make sure you plan accordingly. The most uncomfortable part is asking someone you  can trust to watch your animals, but yet not invite them to your wedding. Awkward. Sometimes a trustworthy neighbor is a good option since they may already know your pets. There are also boarding facilities that you can drop your pets off to if that will suffice for you. Make sure you research each facility to be sure your four legged family members will have their needs met.

24. Prepare Your Bridal Party

Your bridal party should be your group that will help with making sure you get to enjoy your evening. Give them tasks like: saving you from unwanted conversations or dramatic situations, make sure people are dancing and having fun, drinking responsibly in order to last the whole night and have more fun! These are your closest friends and family members. Your emotions and experience should be one of their priorities. You should prepare to have an earnest conversation with your bridal party and let them know they are your first line of defense as well as your team for fun.

25. Getting Your Groomsmen In Order

It is all too common to have at least one groomsmen that is unreliable or unorganized. You may even have several in your bridal party. There is nothing wrong with that, so don't kick them out of the group just yet. A great way to make sure that person is showing up on time and even picking up their Suit/Tux on time is to assign a responsible family member or bridal party member the task with overseeing their responsibilities also. Lets face it, some times people still need to be parented no matter how old they are. You're going to have a lot of stress factors already, assign someone else to handle this one ahead of time.

26. Keeping Your Bridesmaids In Order

It seems to be that the ladies are usually the most organized and reliable when it comes to preparation for your big day. You're less likely to have to constantly remind your bridesmaids the way you will with the groomsmen. However, once the party starts the tricky part is making sure they are keeping themselves together. You're ladies may be very well put together and you won't have to worry about anything. But just in case, it's better to be safe than sorry. With all of the emotions flying around all day mixed with the consumption of alcohol and excitement, you're going to want to avoid any train wrecks. It is not a bad idea to also assign a family member to oversee the ladies from a distance to ensure there is some supervision if necessary. It is highly recommended to prepare your bridesmaids ahead of time and encourage them to have fun, but not to overindulge. At least not until the after party. If you just express to them that you don't want anything ruining your special day, they're more likely to take it to heart. Sometimes they just need a little reminder of how important this is for you.

27. Bridesmaids And Groomsmen Gifts

Your bridesmaids and grooms are already honored for simply being an important part of your big day. Giving them an actual gift is customary, but not totally necessary. If you have a great bridal party,

they won't expect you to give them a gift and
extend your budget out any more than necessary
just for them. However, it
is nice to give them some
sort of a token to remind
them of how special they
are and what a great
experience your wedding
was. So, if you're
planning on giving them a
gift, go as affordable as possible. Don't worry
about buying them something cool and expensive.
Trying to be clever can be costly. You don't need to
engrave cuff links or buy fancy pearls that they will
most likely only wear once or twice. Instead, think
about creating something that is more personal like
a hand crafted object or even a personalized letter
telling them why you selected them to be a part of
your big day. I had DJ'd a wedding once where the
groom crafted a wooden tool holder with a carrying
handle for each groomsman. He presented it to

them with a six pack of their favorite beer that fit right in it perfectly. It was very creative and cost effective.

28. Shop Smart

Sign up for specials online and always be on the lookout for coupons redeemable at places like Hobby Lobby or Michael's. Especially if you want to prepare your own decorations. A lot of times these stores will offer a 10% or even 20% off entire purchase, so always be on the lookout.

29. Look Out For Seasonal Sales For Decorations

If you've given yourself plenty of time to plan your wedding, you could come across many after season sales. After fall, all of the fall decor at most department stores get marked down or go to a clearance rack. The same goes for most holidays and seasons. Start stocking up right away to save extra money when you get to putting your decorations together.

30. Wedding Resale Events

Every year many brides and grooms have a lot of stuff left over from their wedding day and they don't know what to do with it all. Search for wedding resale events in your area and you could pick up a lot of decor and extra small items at a very reasonable price. Remember to take good care of your items from your big day in order to also try and sell them to another lucky couple looking to stay budget friendly.

31. Pinterest

There are a lot of Pinterest boards designated to DIY wedding information as well as wedding suggestions. If you have not already done so, you should create a Pinterest board right away. This will allow you to start putting together ideas you find for decorating, dresses, food, cakes, etc and keep them all in one place. You'll have fun browsing all of the great images and creative ideas from all over designated to wedding ideas. You can reference back to your Pinterest board throughout your entire planning process for a reminder of all the great ideas you've had along the way. Keep in mind also that not everything will be as easy as it looks online. You may come across something that looks perfect for your big day but may be quite the task to put it together. So as long as you have realistic expectations, Pinterest can be a very fun tool to add extra fun and creativity for your big day.

32. Shop On Etsy!

etsy.com You can find a lot of great deals on creative decorations, faux floral arrangements, bridesmaids and groomsmen gifts, and even dresses. It's easy and affordable. Simple as that.

33. Designate Tasks To People

There are a lot of small responsibilities leading up to and even on the day of your wedding that you should not have to be bogged down by. If you're not hiring a professional wedding planner to handle these tasks, don't be afraid to recruit family members. Even for tasks as simple as: making sure the gifts get to the hotel safely, bringing boxes for remaining cake or your top cake layer, cutting the cake for your guests (some facilities charge a fee for cake cutting), even designated drivers for getting guests to their destinations after the reception.

34. Don't Hire A Friend Or Family Member

You're putting a lot in to planning a day that you and your family and friends will remember for the rest of your lives. Even though you may have some friends or family members that have hobbies of photography, playing music, or even party planning, it is best to trust the professionals. A professional wedding service provider will be more likely to have the experience dealing with unforeseen situations that could potentially arise and they will be more adept to handle things quickly and quietly. Also, wouldn't you want your friends and family to enjoy your big day as well? If you "hire" them they still may enjoy themselves and maybe even a little too much, then fail to do the job that will meet up with your expectations. Although you can assign some family members tasks for your big day, it is strongly discouraged to allow someone that isn't a professional to handle major elements such as, DJing/Hosting, Wedding Planning, Videography, Photography, Bar Service, or Catering. Trust the professionals.

35. Address Labels For Bridal Shows

Attending bridal shows during your wedding planning process will help you not only save money but also find some great new ideas. Bridal shows can feel overwhelming and a little chaotic at times. Print address labels with your information on them that includes your Name, Email, Phone Number, and wedding date. You can get some affordable templates at any office store that will allow you to create them yourself. Printing address labels will save you a lot of time when talking to so many wedding professionals.

36. Service Specials (Bridal Show Specific)

When talking to great wedding professionals at a bridal show, don't be afraid to ask what specials they are running during the bridal show and if they will still honor it after the show. Most wedding professionals will be offering a bridal show special in order to give the attendees of the show more incentive for taking the time to come and talk to them.

37. Watch Out For The "Sales Pitch" (Bridal Show Specific)

Beware of "The Best Deal Ever" pitches or the "You have to book today" scare tactics at these shows. If it seems too good to be true, it just might end up being your worst nightmare. Some companies will make sure they send their best "salesman" or "saleswoman" that is skilled in the art of closing the deal. If you don't feel totally comfortable, remember, you don't have to book. You have plenty of time still, don't be pressured in to making a decision. Simply follow your instincts. It is also a good idea to make sure your fiancé is there with you to ensure you make decisions together.

38. Bring Backup To Bridal Shows

Have a friend, family member, or someone in your bridal party even, come with you to bridal shows. The more people you bring, the more questions you will be able to come up with for wedding professionals and more opinions to help you decipher through all of the chaos. Task someone with you to "Save" you if you get sucked into a conversation or situation you don't feel comfortable with. Come up with a signal for that person to recognize so they can step in and interrupt the conversation with an excuse to leave the area.

39. Requesting Recommendations On Social Media

If at all possible, try to avoid requesting recommendations on social media for wedding professionals. Primarily

because you will end up getting bombarded with suggestions, recommendations, friend requests, and private messages from and about everyone under the sun that has or could possibly do something for a wedding. Everyone will be wanting to give you "the best deal" and claim they're "the best around". The best way to find a professional is to search google, wedding wire, the knot, and other prominent wedding oriented websites then research their applicable websites and social media to get a feel for their services. If you decide to ask for recommendations on social media, still do your research. You should avoid basing your decision solely on how many of your "friends" have recommended someone or some thing for your big day.

40. Sticking To A 5 Hour Reception

Some people want to "Party All Night Long". All too often this is an unrealistic expectation when it

comes to your wedding reception. A 5 hour block is
the standard time frame
for a wedding reception.
It is the perfect amount
of time for your guests
of time for your guests
to: mingle during cocktail
hour, enjoy a nice
dinner, then have fun
with dancing and
entertainment. Your
wedding day will be one of the most memorable
days you will ever experience, you don't need to
have all of those memories at your reception.
Adding extra hours to your reception is more costly
than simply going out for an after party drink with
your closest friends and family to finish the night off.
When adding extra hours, you will need to consider
extra hall costs, paying for the bar to stay open and
extra to keep staff on site. Instead, it is much more
cost effective if you rent some sort of shuttle bus,
limo bus, or even a designated driver to take all of

those who are interested to an after party bar for more celebrating.

41. Ending Your Reception At The Perfect Hour

If your reception ends at a later hour, you're likely to have more guests leave earlier than you would like to. Your wedding day can be a long day for your guests too. From the time they have to spend on getting ready, travel, or assisting with tasks. On the other hand if your reception ends at an earlier hour, it may be too early and the energy of your guests may have just begun to get exciting. A recommended hour to end your reception is either 10pm or 11pm. You'll still have time to go out afterwards and enjoy yourself even more if you're up for it.

42. Choosing The Right Reception Site

If you don't have your dream wedding location already selected, here are some factors to think about when choosing the right receptions site. Can it accommodate your guest list comfortably without all of the tables being packed closely together? Do they have in house catering or are you allowed to bring in your own caterer? How easy is it for out of town guests to find your facility? Can you imagine yourself walking in to the room with hundreds of your friends and family cheering for you? If it feels right, go with it. And of course, you're going to want to check in to all the pricing options and restrictions for the facility. But most importantly, go with your gut. You only get one shot to do it right.

43. Minimize The Time Between Ceremony And Reception

By having your reception immediately following your ceremony, you're allowing all of your guests to follow an easier timeline. When you have a gap of time between your ceremony and reception, your potentially risking that most of your out of town guests will not know what to do. Some may even try to go to the reception site right away only to find they will not be allowed to enter the facility. A lot of facilities will keep their doors locked till about 15-30 minutes prior to your scheduled "guest arrival time". Nobody wants to sit in a parking lot and wait. If you're wanting time to go on a limo ride between the ceremony and reception, keep in mind the bridal party typically does this with the bride and groom during the Cocktail Hour. Remember, this is a long day for your guests as well. The longer the day for your guests, the sooner more of them are likely to leave the reception.

44. Keep Your Ceremony Music Simple

A great way to save some money in your budget is to simplify your ceremony music option. When it comes to ceremony ambiance, it is typically already beautiful because you're getting married. As long as you have the ability to project some instrumental music for guest arrival, there are only a few songs that need to be played during a ceremony. If you hire a DJ, quartet, or professional musician, you may be paying more than necessary. This is where you can really save on entertainment without it effecting too much of your guests experience.

45. Ceremony Programs

It is customary to hand out programs for your wedding ceremony to guests as they arrive to the ceremony space. This can become an unnecessary additional cost and an added responsibility you'll need to recruit someone to handle. Most of your guests won't even notice if you decide to not do a program for your ceremony. A typical wedding reception for modern day brides and grooms is about 20-30 minutes. Your guests should be able to follow along for that amount of time. Forgo a program and you'll save some extra time and money by not having to hire someone to create them or even putting the time in yourself to create and print them. If you decide to do a program for your ceremony, another great tip is to try and keep it to one page. You'll save on printing costs.

46. Ceremony And Reception In Same Location

There are many facilities that can accommodate a ceremony and reception in the same location. By having your ceremony and reception together in the same location, you're more likely to save on your budget by combining the cost of both in one package. Also, your guests will be able to move from one element to another much easier.

47. Minimal Decoration Facilities

Finding a reception site that is already beautiful or has permanent structures and decorations in place will allow you to save on decorating costs. The facilities that are beautiful enough to avoid decorations and/or already have decorations in place will most likely have absorbed these costs in their rental rates in order to be more cost effective for brides and grooms.

48. Decorating Time Frames

The last thing you'll be wanting to do after a fun wedding reception full of drinking dancing and more, is think about taking out the trash. Ask your reception facility about clean up responsibilities to figure out whether or not you'll need to designate someone in charge of that. Most facilities have a cleaning fee that could potentially be assessed if a mess is left afterwards.

49. Reception Parking

On site parking is always a plus when deciding on a facility. This will avoid upsetting your guests with the inconvenience of walking a long distance all dressed up. You should also find out how man parking spaces are available to ensure that all of your guests will have a space on site to park. If parking is off site or a distance, does the facility offer a shuttle to accommodate your guests?

50. Clean Up Questions To Ask

If you are not hiring a professional decorator for your wedding reception, there are a few things you'll need to keep in mind. You'll need to find out if your facility allows a certain time frame or a specified amount of time for decorating purposes. It is best to be aware if your facility has any regulations you'll need to follow when hanging decorations and if they have equipment to assist you such as ladders or step stools available. After your reception you'll want to be aware if you will need to have everything cleared out that evening or if you can coordinate to pick things up another time and plan accordingly.

51. Hotel Accommodations For Guests

Some of your guests will be traveling from out of town. Finding a facility that is close to hotels that can accommodate those guests is very important.

Most hotels will allow you to reserve a block of rooms at a discounted rate to allow your guests the option to save some extra money on their travels. You'll want to reserve that block right away as chances are that your wedding may not be the only one that weekend. Get confirmation from the hotel on how many rooms you have available in order to ensure they don't overbook their hotel and not have those rooms available. Some hotels will also provide a shuttle to and from your reception site that will be scheduled at certain times.

52. Request To Customize Your Beverage Options

Most facilities you visit will have pre set bar packages for you to choose from. However, many of those packages can be customized to save you money. When paying for beverages for each guest, consider opting for a Beer and Wine and soda pop package only for your guests, then request 1 or 2 bottles of liquor for the bride and groom/bridal party or immediate family only. Not all facilities will accommodate, but it doesn't hurt to ask if you can customize your bar options. The Beer and Wine only package will also help assist keeping your guests from getting out of control or overindulging. Also, inquire if they have reduced package pricing for underage guests and/or non-drinkers.

53. Catering Options

Choose the best catering style that meets your expectations. There are three most common styles of catering, family style, buffet, and plated meals. Whatever your preferences are, remember not to "over do" it. Of course you want to stray away from the "typical wedding food" feel because it's your day and you deserve the best. Keeping it simple and adding a few extra elements that are personal to you is a great way to approach your dinner menu for your wedding. Try to avoid selecting all of the delicious specialty items you like during your tasting. Oh yea, make sure you do a tasting! Most caterers have their own recipes and certain ways that they prepare dishes for large groups of people. It is important to make sure you like the way your caterer prepares the food for your wedding day. Honestly, your guests will enjoy whatever food you provide for them, and as long as their bellies are full, that's what matters the most when it comes to the food.

54. Kids Meals

Most kids under the age of 10 (and honestly some adults too) either don't want the full meal or won't eat all of it anyways. Ask your caterer if they prepare kids meals for anyone under a certain age. A lot of caterers will offer a kids meal option

like chicken tenders, french fries, etc. for a reduced rate per child.

55. Rehearsal Dinner

Your rehearsal dinner is for all of your immediate family, bridal party, and some close friends to come together and go over any last minute details for the big day. Two major tips combined into one for this element are 1. Don't Party Too Much - you've got a big day ahead of you tomorrow. By now you've already had your bachelor and bachelorette party, this shouldn't be treated as round two. 2. Have a potluck - You can rent a smaller space, or ask a friend/family member to allow you to use their house instead of going to a restaurant. Have everyone coming to bring a dish for people to snack on. This will save you a lot of money by not having to pay for everyone's meals and gratuity as well at a restaurant.

56. Shopping Local

When searching online for wedding professionals, wedding companies, and wedding services, you will likely see sponsored ads from companies all around the country. You may even see ads from local companies or service providers that are trying to "stand out". It is recommended that you skip past any sponsored ads whether local or otherwise and look into the businesses in your area that have a great reputation without paying for advertisements. Hiring a company or service from outside of the area may add more possible opportunity for things to go wrong. Most local wedding professionals are great people that care about what they do in their town. You're more likely to meet someone that will have similar interests or experiences and they may give you a discount simply because they like you and want to take care of you personally. You'll receive a more personalized experience.

57. Book Your Desired Services As Soon As Possible

The major elements of your wedding like Facility, Photographer, DJ, and Caterer have limited availability when it comes to booking. Also, keep in mind that the better the service, the more "in demand" they will be. To ensure you are getting the best possible professionals for your big day, book with your desired services right away. Don't wait till 3 months before your wedding to hire a dj or photographer, you will likely miss out on some great talent. It's not uncommon to book your desired wedding professionals between 12 - 18 months in advance.

58. Interview Your Wedding Professionals

Once you have done your research and narrowed down your candidates, make sure that you take the time to interview the wedding professionals you are wanting to hire for your big day. You can't always get a feel for a person or a company simply by reading online information and corresponding through email or phone calls. By sitting down with your desired wedding professionals, you allow them to describe in more detail what you can expect from their services and you're less likely to have any "surprises" along the way. Keep an open mind and be aware of any red flags that may come up. Don't be afraid to ask questions and don't be afraid to say no. There are a lot of talented "sales professionals" out there, so be aware of what you want and expect ahead of time and you'll be less likely to just be sold on something based on false promises.

59. Research Your Wedding Professionals

There will be a lot of people giving you referrals of friends, family members, or even people they've seen in

action. It is important to research reviews, testimonials, pricing, experience, and professionalism in order to weed out the service providers that will not fit your expectations, level of standards, or even your personality.

60. Asking For Discount On Services

Not every service providers will honor or even offer discounts. However, if you don't ask you'll never know. The key to asking for discounts on services is being honest and reasonable with your request. A lot of wedding professionals will offer a 10% discount for one reason or another. So it doesn't hurt to ask, you may just save some money. Inquire about military discounts if applicable. If you're looking at a golf club or lodge of some sort for your reception, ask if they give discounts for any family that may also be a member at the facility.

61. Ask For Recommendations From Professionals

Professionals work well with other professionals. Many times your photographer or facility will have a favorite DJ or caterer they work with. Getting these recommendations will not only ensure that you will be more likely to have another great professional, but the recommended professional may also offer a discount for the referral (although not guaranteed). Simply because they want to work with those that they enjoy working with.

62. Service Referral Discounts

Don't be afraid to ask your wedding service professionals if they give discounts for referrals. During your planning process, you're likely to come across other brides and grooms looking for something you may already have or a service you've already hired. Ask your service professionals if they have an incentive program in place for if you refer other brides and grooms to them and if they offer any additional discounts after booking those referrals. Of course a professional wedding service provider would want you to refer them based on their abilities and reputation alone, but it doesn't hurt to bring them extra business if it will also save you on your budget. Not all wedding professionals will offer this extra price break, but it does not hurt to ask.

63. Avoid Getting Referred For A Payout

I mentioned previously that you can get recommendations from other professionals, encouraged you to meet with your professional options, and also to do your research. All of those things go hand in hand when it comes to selecting the best option for you. Just because a wedding service provider refers another wedding service provider, that does not always mean that they are the best quality. An insider tip of the wedding industry is that some companies offer "kickbacks" or monetary referral programs to other wedding professionals in order to get more referrals for their business. It is always recommended to get a second and even third opinion on your important services to ensure that you are actually getting a quality recommendation or referral and not just being used for someone to make more money in the wedding industry. It is definitely a thing that you should be aware of. It is also ok if you simply ask if someone is receiving any monetary gain or "Kickback" from any services they recommend.

64. Bundle Deals With Wedding Professionals

These days a lot of wedding companies offer more than one service for brides and grooms. If you come across a company like this, you'll want to ask questions about each service and research each service accordingly. Some people in the wedding industry are just out to make money and take advantage of brides and grooms by offering sub par services only to seem like they are providing more options. What you will need to determine is if the company you're dealing with is passionate about weddings and what they do, or are they just out to make money. Look for any red flags, do your research on each service offered, stick to your expectations, and go with your gut. Do they have a professional work space (office, warehouse, meeting space, etc.) or are they just working out of their house or garage? (There are some professionals that are passionate about what they do but haven't grown enough yet to purchase a professional work space, so go with your gut, do your research, and be aware.) Do they have professional staff or employees that handle each service accordingly? If you're comfortable with who you are hiring for a certain service, and they offer additional services, it can be beneficial to just hire them for that service as well (if you feel comfortable). You'll most likely get a bundled package and can save extra money on your budget. Plus, you will most likely only have to deal with one or two people for several services.

65. Avoid Unnecessary Extra Fees

Read your agreements carefully when hiring wedding service professionals in order to be aware of any extra fees or service charges that you can avoid. If any of your services provide delivery fees (florist, bakery, etc.), try to recruit a family member to take on the task of picking up or dropping off items. Be aware of any additional hour costs and ask if that particular professional has any suggestions on avoiding extra hour costs based on their professional experience. When it comes to decorations like linens or chair covers, ask if they provide a discount if you offer to set them up yourself. Setting up some things yourself can potentially save you hundreds of dollars.

66. Don't Cut Your Entertainment Budget

Keep in mind the biggest thing your guests will remember after your wedding is how much fun they had or did not have on your wedding day. That makes the importance of hiring a professional DJ or Band even that much greater. If you're putting all of this money in to your wedding and planning what is essentially a "party to remember forever" the entertainment element should be held to a very high standard. There are a lot of horror stories out there and most of them involve a poor, unprofessional, or ridiculous DJ that had no idea what they were doing. When shopping around the only question most brides and grooms know to ask is what the cost is. A professional DJ service ranges from $1000-$1600. Anything under that and you're taking a risk on the biggest day of your life. The saying goes "you get what you pay for", and that phrase is in existence for a reason. Do yourself a favor and do your research to find a quality service. You'll thank yourself afterwards.

67. Hiring A Band

If you're a fan of live music then you will absolutely love having a live band at your reception. The experience is very fun and energetic. Make sure you do your due diligence and find a professional band that can accommodate all of your tastes in music, won't take too many breaks, have a professional reputation, won't get too intoxicated, and are not likely to split up before your wedding day. Get a contract written up for the band if they don't already have one ready for you to fill out. That way you can ensure that everything will be more likely to go according to plan. A professional band will be able to provide you a list of songs they are capable of playing as well as "Set Lists" with songs they recommend playing in a certain order to ensure great energy. Try not to be too overbearing with the music selections and allow them to utilize their creative talents.

68. Hiring A DJ With Your Band

It is no secret that bands can create energy that DJs cannot create, and vice versa. Bands are fun and interactive more than most DJs and they can create a visual entertainment element along with the music.

However a large amount of people fail to realize that bands take breaks and music still needs to be played. A lot of bands will just plug in an iPod on shuffle during their breaks. When that's the case, there's no constant flow of music (beat matching), it will most likely just be random songs, and the sound quality will most likely be sub par with no one to maintain the levels of each song. Also, although bands are great at singing and playing a lot of your favorite hits, there are a lot of songs they won't be able to play, they are limited on their requests, and it is unlikely they are capable of handling all of the appropriate announcements to keep the flow of your timeline going smoothly. Hiring a DJ with the band will allow your guests to still make requests, you'll be able to hear a more wide variety of music, and the DJ can host the evening and allow the band to focus on their strong point which is performing great music. If you're hiring a Band and also a DJ, most DJs will give you an extreme discount on their services since they will be doing less work when it comes to playing the music for your reception.

69. Make Sure To Hire A Professional DJ

With today's access to music and digital equipment, there are a lot of "Wedding DJs" out there that have a limited understanding on the importance of a wedding. BEWARE of the "one man show" type of Wedding DJ that just does it for a hobby. There are reputable DJ Service companies out there that have contingency plans in place for all elements that could potentially go wrong leading up to and even on the day of your wedding. Hiring a professional will save you a lot of stress and time.

70. Music Requests On Your Invitations

A lot of brides and grooms want to include a song request section on their invitations they send out in order to allow their guests to give their input on what music they would like to hear at the reception. This can be helpful if you go with a lower quality or budget dj service and you do not know what to expect from them. One thing that most brides and grooms don't consider is that you may just be opening a door that can create more issues than necessary. There are always going to be random requests that won't fit the energy or the expectations of the evening. You also don't want to upset anyone if their song doesn't get a chance to get played for whatever reason. From the perspective of a professional DJ, it's best to let the professionals handle it and allow your guests to just enjoy themselves.

71. Hire A Wedding Planner

There are a lot of things you can do on your own through the planning process, and there are also a lot of elements you can designate to friends/family members. However, if you really want things to go smoothly, you should definitely look in to hiring a wedding planner. The best way to save money when hiring a wedding planner is to hire them for just the day of coordination. There are a lot of things that could go wrong on your big day, there are even more responsibilities that have to be overseen. If you really want things to go as smooth as you've imagined, a professional wedding planner handling the day of coordination for you will take care of everything! They'll even handle things without you even knowing they've been handled in order to ensure you are not exposed to any unnecessary stress on your big day. Of course there are wedding planner options that allow them to help you throughout the entire planning process as well. It all depends on how much responsibility you want to take on yourself or how much you don't want to deal with or worry about.

72. Hire A Professional Photographer.

With the increasingly affordable and accessibility to somewhat quality camera equipment, newbie photographers and image enthusiasts pop up every day. We already went over not

hiring a friend or family member. You will also want to avoid hiring a photographer that is not already skilled at wedding photography and wedding etiquette. Capturing a professional image is only a fraction of the work a professional wedding photographer brings to the table. They also have to be able to rally up the appropriate people for shoots, have an eye for a great shot, quick reflexes for those random memorable moments that pop up, and know how to touch up and edit photographs after the wedding in order to provide you with the perfect memories captured with quality. You will also want someone that has a calming a professional demeanor. I have personally witnessed several "photographers" literally yelling at guests to "get out of the way". This does nothing but irritate the guests simply to get a good photograph. A good photographer will know how to deal with these situations without being abrasive. You will thank yourself later if you hire a professional wedding photographer.

73. Photographer Time Frame

Depending on what photographer you use, and what type of service you decide on from them, they may be with you at the early hours of the morning. You are definitely going to want to capture the entire day if at all possible, but you will need to be mindful of your evening timeline. If you start your photographer early and then plan for them to leave early, your events at your reception (cake cutting, dances, bouquet garter, anniversary dance, dollar dance, etc.) can potentially be rushed to be done all at once. Some people think that this is ok because then you can just party and dance the rest of the night. However, most of your guests will just be sitting around the entire time for cocktail hour, dinner, and through all of your events. After all of that, they may not want to stick around because they've sat for so long, or they may have already left. A great suggestion is to plan your photographer's time accordingly so they capture your reception all the way up to the last hour or hour and a half. This will allow for your reception events to be spread out with dancing and fun in between them. Your guests will enjoy themselves even more.

74. Limiting Your Videographer Time

If you have not thought about having a videographer at your wedding, it is highly recommended. Pictures are great to capture moments, but video captures so much more. If you are planning on hiring a videographer for your wedding, ask if they have a limited package. Consider just the ceremony or only an hour or two at the reception. If you've hired professionals, you are likely to remember a lot of the fun and dancing at the reception, so you may not need most of that to be captured. Some videographers offer single shooter packages with multiple camera angles.

Keep in mind one person can only capture so much, so a second shooter will be able to capture even more. However, having a stationary camera for one angle and then a single shooter for extra angles of coverage area can be more cost effective.

75. Hiring a makeup specialist.

If you are already comfortable doing your own make up or trust a friend or family member with the task of handling the make up process for your big day, you will save some extra money.

However a professional make up artist is likely to be skilled with colors and applying make up in ways that you may not have thought about in order for your pictures to be even that much more perfect. If you are thinking about hiring a professional make up specialist, make sure they give you a trial session to allow you to fully understanding of their abilities. That way you can compare and decide if you really want to hire a makeup specialist or simply do it on your own. You will also be able to feel comfortable knowing their process, their abilities, and a little bit about them in general. Make sure they are reliable, professional, and have a great demeanor that all of your ladies (moms, bridesmaids, grandparents, etc.) are going to get a long with. Go with your gut.

76. Ditch The Limo/Party Bus

Typically after the ceremony, the bride, groom, and bridal party go with the photographer for pictures somewhere while all of your guests rally to the reception site for the cocktail hour. If your ceremony and reception are all in one place, the limo or party bus rental is unnecessary. However, if you're traveling from one place to another, most brides and grooms think it is necessary to have a limousine or party bus to transport them. The most common reason for this is because they want to start (or even continue) drinking during the commute from ceremony to reception. There is nothing wrong with wanting to do that at all. This tip is not to say that you shouldn't rent a limo or party bus, but instead shed light on an alternative that can be more cost effective for your budget. A great suggestion is to simply rent a town car or something classy for the commute. Then if you want a beverage, just stop at a local pub, you may just get a free drink or shot since it is your wedding day. Another option is instead of renting a town car or classy car, find out if any friend or family member owns a classic style car that would look amazing and be also be perfect for wedding photos. An important thing to remember is that you are going to have plenty of access to beverages at your reception, you will most likely save money if you plan ahead of time to drink responsibly.

77. Purchasing Suit Vs Renting Tux For Groom & Groomsmen

More modern day brides and grooms have been opting to be less formal than previous generations when it comes to Bridal Wear. Many Mens Formal Wear Companies have Tuxedo Rental options as well as Suits for sale. Don't be afraid to simply ask if they have any specials on Suits for weddings. At many places, you will find that purchasing a suit will be around the same price range as renting a Tuxedo for the groom and groomsmen. The only drawback to this is that when renting a Tuxedo, you get all the fixings like shirt, tie, shoes, suspenders, etc. However, the upside to purchasing a suit is that the groom and the groomsmen will now have a great suit to wear to other formal occasions in the future. Whatever your preference is, make sure you shop around and see who has the best options for you and your budget.

78. Don't Overdo The Cake Or Cupcakes.

The wedding cake is one
of the anticipated elements
of any wedding. Most of
your guest will enjoy some
of that delicious dessert
you spent a lot of money
on. However, there will be
many guests that will

either not want cake, can't have cake, or even just
forget about the cake. I've seen many weddings
end that have more cake or cupcakes than they
know what to do with. It is my personal
recommendation that you lower your serving
options when it comes to your cake/cupcake
purchases. Unless you want to provide your guests
with extra cake to take home with them. It is a great
way to save a little on your budget. After being
involved in over 1000 weddings I can honestly say

that I have never witnessed any wedding ever run out of cake or cupcakes. There is typically a lot left over and the family has to encourage any remaining guests to take some with them.

79. Real or Faux Floral Arrangements

This tip is all up to your own opinion. If you can find some great looking faux floral arrangements that meet your expectations, you will definitely save some additional costs on your budget. You can then try to resell them after your wedding day to another lucky bride and possibly recoup some of your expenses. However, having real flowers instead of faux flowers will create a great aroma throughout your ceremony and reception site and give a more natural appeal.

80. Use Bigger Flowers In Bouquets

Having a big beautiful bouquet will make for some amazing pictures. If this is the look you are going for, a great way to save some cost on bouquets and even floral arrangements in general is to opt for bigger flowers. Having bigger flowers usually means that you will use less flowers to get the full bouquet look and save you some cost with the florist you hire.

81. Minimize Your Floral Arrangements

Another great way to save on your floral budget is to limit the amount of floral arrangements necessary for your big day. You can easily just ditch the bridesmaids

bouquets and opt for a wrist corsage. You can also think about going with a store bought tossing bouquet, if you're doing the bouquet toss at all. The best part about the tossing bouquet is the tossing element, it does not necessarily need to be super extravagant.

82. Photo Sharing Apps

There are several photo sharing apps like WedPics that allow all of your guests to take pictures with their smart phones and share them all in one place. This will allow you to capture even more fun from your big day. The only tricky part is making sure all of your guests know how to download the app and login to use it. But you can easily print up an instruction sheet to be placed somewhere and also have your DJ/Host make announcements.

83. Photo Booth Or DIY?

These days it seems that a photo booth is another must have for your wedding planning process. There are dozens of options for photo booths for your wedding day. If you have designated a portion of your budget for photo booth, you can either hire a photo booth service or do it yourself with a simple camera and backdrop. If you hire a professional photo booth service, you'll need to make sure their props are fun and creative, their images are high resolution, it is a service that is more than just a camera on a tripod (you can do that yourself), they provide you with the images after the event, and the prints are high quality paper prints that come out quickly to ensure your guests are having fun. There should also be an attendant at the photo booth at all times. If you decide to do the photo booth yourself, you will most likely save money but you may risk the quality of experience and photos taken. The DIY option is more difficult when trying to provide prints for your guests. You can even set up an instagram image frame prop and have someone use your phones or a designated camera to take pictures of all of your guests. When it comes to photo booth, the more fun the experience, the better!

84. Use Your Photo Booth Prints As Favors

If you are planning on hiring a photo booth company that will also be providing prints, most companies will allow you to customize those prints to match the theme of your wedding. A great tip is to simply use those prints as a favor for your guests take home with them. That way it is personalized to your wedding and it's something that they will want to keep due to having their picture incorporated in it as well. The photo booth company may also even put together a scrap book with extra images inserted in to it and allow your guests to write little messages to you. This scrap book can also double as your guest book. By incorporating the photo booth prints as favors and possibly the scrap book as your guest book, you will be encouraging your guests to have even more fun by participating in the photo booth element.

85. Craft A "DIY" Favor For Your Guests

There are a lot of websites online devoted to guest favors for weddings. A helpful tip would be to take the time to (or dedicate a friend/family member to) create something with affordable materials. It will not only be cost effective, but you will also make it more personal for your guests to enjoy. Some examples are: Cutting and engraving wood "Coasters", anything using Origami, decorated small candles, Plant a flower seed or tree seed in a small dixie cup or something of that size, etc. Hot chocolate kits, or even homemade Jam are also great ideas for guest favors.

86. Trusting The DJ

A Professional Wedding DJ has many responsibilities on top of just playing music and making announcements. One of those many responsibilities is the ability to filter through the random requests that your guests are likely to make. If one of your guests does not like a particular song, or wants to hear a particular song that has not been played yet, they may come up to you and ask you to tell the DJ what to do. Keep in mind when dealing with a large group of people, everyone has their own opinion about music, but it does not mean that all opinions are what is right for the entirety of your guests. It is best to just trust your dj with the responsibilities he or she has for the flow of the evening as well as the level of fun and the energy of all your guests in attendance. A great tip is to just let them do their job instead of listening to your guests. Once you allow one person to have that control, many others will follow along with their own opinion. Remember if you've done your research and chosen the right dj for your big day, you have hired a professional because they are the professional.

87. Have A Detailed Final Planning Meeting With Your DJ

Most DJs are booked approximately between the range of 6 months to a year and a half prior to the big day. You may have had new musical tastes arise, new music has came out, and many elements in your planning process may have changed since you had first met with your DJ. It is always recommended to schedule a very detailed final planning meeting one or two weeks prior to your big day. Any professional DJ should already be doing this. However, if you haven't heard from your dj within 30 days of your wedding date, make sure you reach out to schedule this. That final meeting will not only inform the DJ of all your expectations, but allow you to understand the capabilities of your dj even more. That way when it comes to the day of, you'll have less stress worrying about the music and flow of the evening.

88. Champagne Tip For Toasting

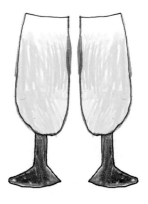

A great way to save some extra money for your wedding reception is to skip the champagne. Not everyone likes champagne and people will toast with whatever you provide for them. All too often you'll be left with full glasses of champagne from those that don't want to drink it, half full bottles, and a lot of money wasted. If you really want that celebratory toast, consider providing champagne for just the head table and immediate family. You also don't need to go all out and get the expensive bubbly. Most people don't know the difference from affordable or expensive champagne, so go affordable if you are getting champagne for toasts.

89. When To Do Toasts/Speeches?

Some people tend to want to do toasts/speeches during or after dinner in order to not have anyone waiting any longer to eat. What they often fail to realize is that if you do toasts/speeches during dinner, there will most likely be a lot of commotion going on (wait staff walking around, dishes clanking, chatter, etc.) and it can be distracting to whoever is giving the toast/speech. Public speaking is not easy for everyone, so it can be stressful for someone to get up and talk in front of a large group of people. If there is too much going on and distracting them from what they want to say, it can heighten the stress and anxiety element even more.

Plus if you plan to do toasts/speeches during dinner, some of your guests may think that they have to stop eating in order to listen to the speeches and then their food will sit there cooling. If you plan for toasts/speeches after dinner, you will need to understand that by this time people have already gotten up from their seats to revisit the bar, go to the bathroom, or just to mingle. It can be a task to get everyones attention and even harder to keep it. The best time to do toasts/speeches is right after the grand entrance. Once the bride and groom enter the room, you have the attention of all of your guests at this point. A welcome speech by a family member would be best to start it off, then best man & maid of honor speeches, anyone else that has planned to say something, right in to the blessing of the meal, then let them eat. This process should only take about 10-15 minutes depending on how long winded some people may be in their speeches.

90. Guests Bringing Their Own Alcohol

Some of your guests will be ready to PAR-TAY and they may opt to bring their own bottle of their favorite alcoholic beverage. Keep in mind most facilities have their own liquor license and this would be in a direct violation of those regulations. And, you've most likely already paid for them to enjoy some adult beverages. Also, if they bring something extra, people might just end up being a "little extra" and create some sort of dramatic occurrence on your big day. It is strongly recommended to encourage your guests to not bring any additional alcohol.

91. Drink Responsibly

Yes, your wedding is the party you have been looking forward to for a long time. You should absolutely enjoy yourself! However, you will remember more, enjoy yourself more, and be much safer if you drink responsibly. We recommend drinking plenty of water in between alcoholic beverages and again make sure you are eating appropriately throughout the day. You also don't want your wedding photos or photos from your wedding guests to be a reflection of you as a hot mess. So pace yourself, you will thank yourself after the wedding. Remember, this is a celebration and not just another night out. You want to be sure to remember all of the special moments that occur throughout the day.

92. Make Sure You Eat!

There will be a lot going on all day long and you are going to be pulled in every different direction from service providers as well as loved ones. With all of this commotion and your emotions being all over the place, it is very easy to forget to eat. We even suggest designating someone to make sure you eat during the day. Especially if you intend on partaking in the consumption of alcoholic beverages. Having something to absorb the alcohol, will ensure you don't overindulge and miss out on any amazing memories. Make sure to snack throughout the day during getting ready time and during pictures.

93. You Don't Need To Go To Every Table

A great way to avoid missing out on the fun that happens at your wedding reception is to not feel like you have to go around to every guest table and thank them for coming. Don't worry, very few of your guests will be offended if you don't visit them at their table. Remember this is your wedding and you should enjoy every minute of it. A great way to prepare your guests not to expect you coming around is to simply say a few words during or after the speeches. My wife and I made sure we did this at our wedding and it was a great way to inform all of our guests. We simply said, "Thank you for coming, you all mean so much to us. If we don't get the opportunity to come around to see all of you, just know how important it is for us that you are here. If at anytime you want to say anything to us, you can most likely find us on the dance floor or the bar". Not that you need to say the same speech verbatim but it will remind the guests that this is your day and you want to enjoy it. They will be more understanding than you think.

94. Taking The Time To Do Assigned Seating

Putting together a seating chart is like putting together a puzzle. If you do not want to deal with it and want to just allow guests to sit anywhere, you are going to want to put out extra chairs and possibly extra tables. Because, guests that don't know each other will most likely just look for an open table, guests that come in groups (2, 3, 4, etc) will want to sit with each other and they will then have to hopefully find a table that still has that many seats still available. The last thing you want is a family of 4 standing around because they can't find a table that has 4 seats at it. This can be uncomfortable for your guests to try and figure things out and most importantly creates additional costs on your wedding budget for the extra seats and tables. Do yourself a favor, put together a seating chart, your guests will be more comfortable.

95. Create A Policy For Children

A lot of people are taking the route of not allowing any children at their wedding to avoid them running around unsupervised. If you are planning on a no children rule, you will want to specify an age range. This  will also keep your guest count lower if you want to save money. You won't have to pay for the kids to attend and, as harsh as it sounds, some families won't be able to attend if they can't bring their kids. If you do allow kids at your wedding you should make it abundantly clear that parents need to supervise their children. A lot of parents just let their kids run wild at weddings (if you are ok with that, then that is completely ok too), and they sometimes get in to things, get hurt, accidentally trip other guests, etc. There are also wedding services out there that you can hire to create a kids section at your reception and they may also provide a wedding sitter for the evening. No matter your outlook on having children at your wedding, the main thing to remember is to make it clear for all of your guests to follow.

96. Purchase A Comfortable Set Of Shoes

Of course you are going to have your formal shoes to be worn for your ceremony and pictures. But, if you're planning on dancing the night away you will want to have a second pair of shoes for comfort and stability. You're going to be on your feet for most of the day, make sure you take care of your feet by having a second more comfortable option of footwear for your reception.

97. Releasing Tables For Dinner

If you are doing a buffet style dinner for your wedding reception, you will absolutely want to have your tables released for the line. Just announcing "dinner is ready" or something like that tends to lead to chaos. There is little to no way of knowing when everyone has had a plate in order to move on with the festivities of the evening. Most professional caterers will release tables themselves because they understand that they are in charge of food service for the reception, it ads a personal touch for their service, and it keeps dinner service in order. Some caterers rely on the DJ/host to release tables. Any good DJ/host will do it if absolutely necessary because they understand the importance of it being done, but this does distract them from their entertainment responsibilities like reading the room, preparing people and elements for the timeline of the evening, handling any last minute requests, and coordinating any "during dinner" activities. If you are relying on your DJ/host to release tables, it is best to number the tables so they can simply announce numbers while they are working on their other responsibilities. Remember to ensure someone is in charge of releasing tables for your dinner service so.

98. Informing Your Guests Of The Food

Add your menu to your table numbers. Your guests will know what to be expecting for food and will more likely go through the buffet line quicker. Then, you won't have to print a menu for each guest and you can save on those additional printing costs.

99. An Alternative To Glass Clinking

It is a common tradition for guests to clink their glasses as a signal that they want the bride and groom to share a kiss with each other. It is a great tradition that has sincerity and love at its core. However, it can become more of a nuisance than anything. The problems that arise from this is that someone will start the clinking of the glasses and it will resonate amongst the guests, you will kiss your betrothed, but not everyone will see it and the clinking will continue for an unnecessary amount of time. You may also get some guests that decide that they think it is funny to start clinking their glass every few minutes and the great heartwarming tradition now becomes an annoying practical joke. You can avoid people clinking their glasses by opting for plasticware, but not if you think that is tacky. There are several other alternatives to the clinking of the glasses that you can use and be creative with. One wedding placed a donation jar at the head table that the guests had to put a donation into the jar and the bride and groom will share a kiss. Another wedding had a hockey buzzer their guests had to press because they were big hockey fans. At our wedding we had a Gong for guests to come up and bang in order for us to kiss. It was much louder than expected so not too many guests came up to ring it. But it still made for a great creative addition to our wedding that nobody had seen done before. Get creative and come up with something that is personal to you and your fiancé and your guests will enjoy it as well.

100. Thank You Cards

Order your thank you cards when you order your invitations. This will save you on extra shipping costs. There are a lot of online companies that will offer

combined discounts on multiple purchases. Then you won't have to still remember to purchase them and wait for the shipping process. This will also allow you to start filling out the thank you cards ahead of time for guests that you know are definitely coming. That way after the wedding you will have less of a task filling out thank you cards to be sent out.

101. Remember to Tip

Being a wedding professional is a service oriented profession. We cater to the needs of many people at our job. It is customary (but for some reason not commonly known) to tip your wedding professionals. Especially if they have done a great job for you on your big day. You do not need to tip everyone you have hired for the day, but you should try to remember to tip your photographer, dj, band, wedding coordinator, bar tenders, caterer (if they don't already include gratuity in their agreement), photo booth attendant, videographer, officiant, and any other key players that have done an outstanding job for your wedding day.

We hope you have enjoyed these wedding planning tips. Even if not all of them pertained to your expectations, budget, and plans for your big day. By the day of your wedding all of your planning should be done and everything should flow together. Keep in mind something may still go wrong, so our final tip is to just go with it and try to enjoy the day as much as possible.

Congratulations again!

39703016R00062